SNAPSHOTS IN HISTORY

THE
KOREAN WAR

America's Forgotten War

by Brian Fitzgerald

THE KOREAN WAR

America's Forgotten War

by Brian Fitzgerald

Content Adviser: Derek Shouba, Adjunct History Professor
and Assistant Provost, Roosevelt University

Reading Adviser: Susan Kesselring, M.A., Literacy Educator,
Rosemount–Apple Valley–Eagan (Minnesota) School District

COMPASS POINT BOOKS
MINNEAPOLIS, MINNESOTA

COMPASS POINT BOOKS

3109 West 50th Street, #115
Minneapolis, MN 55410

Visit Compass Point Books on the Internet at
www.compasspointbooks.com
or e-mail your request to
custserv@compasspointbooks.com

For Compass Point Books
Jennifer VanVoorst, Jaime Martens, XNR Productions, Inc.,
Catherine Neitge, Keith Griffin, and Carol Jones

Produced by White-Thomson Publishing Ltd.
Tel.: 0044 (0)1273 403990
210 High Street, Lewes BN7 2NH

For White-Thomson Publishing
Stephen White-Thomson, Brian Krumm, Amy Sparks, Tinstar Design
Ltd. *www.tinstar.co.uk*, Derek Shouba, Joselito F. Seldera, Bill Hurd,
and Timothy Griffin

Library of Congress Cataloging-in-Publication Data
Fitzgerald, Brian, 1972–
The Korean war: America's forgotten war / by Brian Fitzgerald.
     p. cm. — (Snapshots in history)
  Includes bibliographical references and index.
  ISBN 0-7565-1625-0 (hardcover)
 1. Korean War, 1950–1953—United States. 2. Truman, Harry S.,
1884–1972. I. Title. II. Series.
  DS919.F59 2006
  951.904'2—dc22   2005027156

THE KOREAN WAR

CONTENTS

A Fast Path to War

Saturday, June 24, 1950, was a busy day for U.S. President Harry Truman. In the morning, he had flown from Washington, D.C., to Baltimore, Maryland, to dedicate the city's new airport. From there, he continued on to his family home in Independence, Missouri. There, he hoped to enjoy a relaxing weekend with his family. Truman was tired from the long day of travel and the hot summer weather. He was sitting in his library when the phone rang at about 9:20 P.M. Secretary of State Dean Acheson was on the line. He told President Truman:

> *Mr. President, I have very serious news. The North Koreans have invaded South Korea.*

The attack had begun more than six hours earlier. Because of the time difference, the invasion actually began about 4 A.M. Korea time on June 25. The South Koreans were taken completely by surprise. Many troops had been given time off to return home to harvest their rice crop. Others were held in reserve many miles from the border, so the force defending the country's northern border was at one-third its usual size.

The South Koreans stood little chance against the invasion force of 90,000 well-trained troops. Soviet-built T-34 tanks streamed across the border. North Korean pilots in Soviet YAK fighter planes attacked airfields and other key targets in the South. Much of the South Korean army was destroyed or in retreat. The North Korean troops marched quickly toward Seoul, the capital of South Korea.

South Korean troops marched to the front lines to battle North Korean invaders during the early days of the war.

Truman knew the invasion was a serious problem for the United States. At the time, the United States was in the early stages of the Cold War. This long period of tension with communist nations, mainly the Soviet Union, lasted nearly four decades. The Korean peninsula contributed to this tension: North Korea was a communist country supported by the Soviets, and South Korea had a democratic government backed by the United States.

Truman feared that a North Korean takeover of South Korea would inspire communist nations around the globe to invade their neighbors. He reasoned that the failure to stop similar advances by Nazi Germany and Japan a decade earlier had led to World War II. Now Truman believed the United States needed to come to the aid of its ally, South Korea, to prevent a third world war.

The president was back in Washington on the evening of June 25. He met with his top advisers, including Secretary Acheson. All agreed that North Korea had to be stopped. The United Nations (U.N.) had already taken action. A few hours earlier, the U.N. Security Council had voted to order North Korea to stop its invasion and withdraw its troops. The resolution passed by a vote of 9-0.

THE ROLE OF THE UNITED NATIONS

The United Nations is an international organization that grew out of a worldwide desire for long-term peace after World War II. The main goal of the United Nations is to resolve problems between nations before the tension leads to all-out war. The Korean War marked the first time the United Nations stepped in to aid a nation against an invading force.

But North Korea ignored the demand and continued its advance through the South. On June 27, the United Nations passed a resolution to defend South Korea from its invaders.

Secretary of State Dean Acheson (left) and President Truman worked together to shape U.S. strategy for the Korean War.

U.S. B-26 bombers attacked railroad yards and other North Korean positions.

Truman also acted quickly. Earlier in the day, he had told members of the U.S. Congress that he had already approved the use of the U.S. Air Force and

Navy to help defend South Korea. Truman knew that he did not have the power to start a war without the approval of Congress. Because of this, he avoided the word *war* when discussing Korea. Instead, he referred to U.S. involvement as a police action.

On June 28, 1950, Seoul fell to the North Korean army. The same day, U.S. B-26 and B-29 bombers made their first assaults on North Korean targets.

In the blink of an eye, the United States found itself in the middle of a battle on the other side of the world. For the first time, the United Nations' mission of keeping peace around the globe would be put to the test. Over the next three years, the "police action" in Korea would claim the lives of more than 36,900 U.S. troops. At least 3,000 soldiers from the other U.N. countries that came to South Korea's aid would also die. And as many as 2 million Chinese troops and Korean soldiers and civilians would lose their lives during the fighting.

A MISSED OPPORTUNITY

The Soviet Union could have delayed the United Nations' entry into the Korean War. As a member of the U.N. Security Council, the Soviets could have voted against supporting South Korea. But months earlier, the Soviets had boycotted the Security Council because the United Nations would not recognize the communist nation of China as a member. Therefore, the Soviets were not there to vote on the war resolution.

Drawing the Line

Chapter

2

The line that marked the border between North and South Korea was not a natural boundary like a river or a mountain range. It also was not a spot that separated people of different races, languages, or customs. The dividing line was the 38th parallel. A parallel is an imaginary circle around Earth that runs in the same direction as the equator. This line was chosen during the final days of World War II for no reason other than that it roughly cut the country in half.

From 1910 to the end of World War II, Korea had been a single country under Japanese control. During World War II, the United States and the Soviet Union worked as allies to defeat their common enemies, chiefly Germany and Japan. But as the war neared its end, the United States grew troubled by the Soviets. American

leaders worried that the Soviets would try to spread communism to other countries by grabbing as much land as possible before the end of the war.

On August 8, 1945—just two days after the United States dropped an atomic bomb on Hiroshima, Japan—the Soviet Union declared war on Japan. Thousands of Soviet troops streamed over the Russian border into the Japanese-held territory of Manchuria, a region in northeastern China. They rapidly advanced through the territory and moved close to the northern border of Korea.

Soviet soldiers guarded a railroad station in the Manchurian city of Harbin after their August 1945 invasion.

15

Government leaders in the United States feared that the Soviets would overtake the entire Korean peninsula. American military leaders called an emergency late-night meeting on August 10, 1945. Two U.S. Army colonels, Dean Rusk and Charles Bonesteel, were assigned to find an acceptable dividing line in Korea. Rusk and Bonesteel studied a map of the area to find the best point to split the country. They needed only 30 minutes to make their choice—the latitude line at the 38th parallel. The northern half of Korea would be occupied by the Soviets, and U.S. troops would occupy the southern half.

American officials sent the plan to the Soviets, who agreed to the dividing line. In their haste to reach an agreement, neither side bothered to consult with Korean leaders about the divide. Soviets troops would accept the Japanese surrender north of the 38th parallel; U.S. troops would accept their surrender south of the line. On September 2, 1945, the Soviet army stopped its march into Korea at the 38th parallel as promised. Six days later, U.S. troops arrived in South Korea. Crowds cheered as the troops entered Seoul to accept the formal surrender from the Japanese. For the next three years, 50,000 U.S. troops would occupy South Korea.

The boundary at the 38th parallel was meant to be temporary. The United States and the Soviet Union had agreed that Korea would be united under a single government. But they did not specify how the type of government would be selected or who its leaders would be.

In November 1947, the United Nations called for a nationwide election to unite Korea once and for all. The plan called for all foreign troops to be removed from the area once the new government was in place. However, the growing tension between the United States and the Soviet Union would make it impossible for the two Koreas to become one again.

The people of the Korean capital of Seoul welcomed U.S. troops into their city in September 1945.

On August 15, 1948, the Republic of Korea was officially formed in the area the U.S. refers to as South Korea. Syngman Rhee became the country's first president. However, the Soviet Union would not allow elections in the North and denied U.N. observers entry into the region. On September 9, 1948, the North revealed its new name, the Democratic People's Republic of Korea. Kim Il Sung, a strong supporter of communism, was its new leader.

PRESIDENT SYNGMAN RHEE

The Republic of Korea's first president, Syngman Rhee, was 73 years old at the time of his election. As a young man, he had founded Korea's first daily newspaper. Rhee was a strong supporter of Korean independence from Japan and had been forced to flee from Korea because of his beliefs. He had lived in the United States and earned degrees from Harvard University and Princeton University in the early 1900s.

General Douglas MacArthur sat with Syngman Rhee, South Korea's first president, during a celebration marking the birth of the Republic of Korea on August 15, 1948.

Each new nation refused to recognize the other. Each Korean leader boasted of plans to reunify Korea under his own form of government. President Rhee's plan to unify Korea worried President Truman, who didn't want a full-scale war in Korea. As a result, after the United States withdrew its troops in 1949, the United States refused to supply South Korea with tanks or planes. Military aid was restricted to light artillery and small arms. The United States wanted the Republic of Korea (ROK) army to be strong enough to defend itself but not strong enough to launch a major attack against its northern enemy.

The Soviets seemed to think just the opposite, and they left behind a very different army. They supplied the North Korean People's Army (NKPA) with heavy artillery, fighter planes, and powerful T-34 tanks. NKPA troops were also well-trained. Many were veterans of the battles against the Japanese in Manchuria during World War II.

Throughout the late 1940s, ROK troops in the South and NKPA troops in the North often clashed along the 38th parallel. These small-scale battles hinted at the danger that was brewing in the region. Unfortunately, neither South Korea nor the United States paid enough attention to the warning signs. ◤

A Fight Until the End

Chapter

3

The differences between the two Korean armies became clear with the defeat of the South Korean ROK forces in late June 1950. To meet the communist threat, U.S. General Douglas MacArthur would assume command of U.N. forces in Korea. The legendary general of World War II fame was 70 years old at the time, but he was still as fiery and as confident as ever. When asked about the NKPA's invasion of South Korea, MacArthur boasted:

> *I can handle it with one arm tied behind my back.*

On the fifth day of fighting, June 29, MacArthur flew from his base in Tokyo, Japan, to observe the front line in Korea. From a distant hilltop, MacArthur saw Seoul surrounded by smoke and flames. The once-proud Korean

General Douglas MacArthur (center) made frequent trips to the front line while he was commander of U.N. forces in Korea.

capital had already been overrun by the North Korean NKPA. ROK forces were fleeing the area.

General MacArthur's eight-hour tour of Korea convinced him that the ROK army could not hold out much longer. They needed the support of U.S. and U.N. ground forces, in addition to the air and naval forces already in action. When the general returned to Tokyo, he sent a message to Washington explaining that the situation was grave. The following day, President Truman agreed to send U.S. ground troops to defend South Korea.

GENERAL DOUGLAS MACARTHUR

Douglas MacArthur (1880–1964) is one of the most famous figures in U.S. military history. In addition to his service during the Korean War, he commanded U.S. forces in the Philippines during World War II. He also accepted the formal Japanese surrender on September 2, 1945.

South Korean recruits took a loyalty oath, swearing to fight for the honor of their country. Most were poorly trained, however, and did not have the firepower to match NKPA forces.

MacArthur had about 50,000 men under his command in Japan, but they were spread throughout the country. While those units were being organized for use in Korea, MacArthur ordered a battalion from the 21st Infantry Regiment, 24th Infantry Division into action immediately. The group was nicknamed Task Force Smith, after its commanding officer, Lieutenant Colonel Charles Bradford Smith.

Task Force Smith was certainly not the Army's best-trained or best-equipped unit. Only about one out of every six soldiers in the 440-soldier unit had any combat experience. Many of the unit's soldiers were teenagers who had grown comfortable during assignments in peacetime Japan.

U.S. military leaders hoped the arrival of these U.S. troops would improve the morale of the South Korean troops. At the time, many ROK soldiers would turn and run at the first sign of North Korean tanks. U.S. leaders also hoped that the sight of Americans on the battlefield would terrify the NKPA troops and cause them to stop fighting.

On the evening of June 30, Lieutenant Colonel Smith got the call to get his men ready for their Korean assignment. By 3 A.M., the soldiers of Task Force Smith were on trucks headed to Japan's Itazuke Air Base. The 75-mile (120-km) trip took five hours. A driving rain slowed travel to a crawl. When they arrived, every man was completely soaked. This was the first of many troubles that awaited the task force.

The soldiers boarded C-54 transport planes headed for an airfield near Pusan in southeastern Korea. After landing on Korean soil, Task Force Smith began a difficult, four-day journey to the front line. They traveled in trains and trucks that took them past long lines of refugees and wounded ROK soldiers. At 3 A.M. on July 5, Task Force Smith reached its destination—about 3 miles (5 km) north of a small town named Osan. Joined by artillery troops, they began to prepare for battle.

Bob Roy, a 19-year-old private, recalled the shock of seeing the enemy for the first time:

> *About seven in the morning I decided to open a can of C rations, and that's when we saw the tanks. I just dropped the can ... Nobody told us about any tanks.*

Task Force Smith did not have any antitank mines, and they only had a handful of artillery shells that could cut through tank armor. Shells from U.S. artillery and bazookas simply bounced off the approaching tanks. Over the next three hours, Task Force Smith knocked out only four of the more than 30 NKPA tanks that rolled through the area.

NKPA infantry soon swarmed onto the battlefield. The men of Task Force Smith fought bravely, but they were outnumbered 10 to one. Riflemen did not have enough ammunition, and many ran out. With his men nearly surrounded, Smith gave the order to retreat. The scene was chaos. Many men abandoned their weapons. They also left behind the dead and any wounded who couldn't walk. The NKPA had not turned and run as U.S. military leaders had predicted. The Americans' first battle with their communist foes had been a crushing defeat.

By the time Task Force Smith was in full retreat, the rest of the 24th Infantry Division had arrived in Korea. U.S. General William Dean ordered the men to create defensive lines. Dean set up U.N. headquarters in Taejon, 100 miles (161 km) south of Seoul.

Other U.N. units suffered in battle just as Task Force Smith had. U.N. troops carried outdated weapons, many of them left over from World War II. The inexperienced troops were no match for the well-armed NKPA. The U.N. forces lost ground daily. Along South Korean roadways, they saw scores of refugees. Roads packed with refugees became a familiar sight to U.N. troops as they moved through the battle-scarred country.

The Korean peninsula was located close to China, Japan, and the Soviet Union.

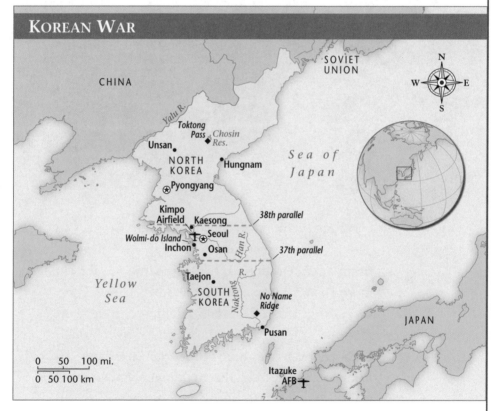

KOREAN WAR

CHINA

SOVIET UNION

N
W · E
S

Yalu R.

Toktong Pass
Chosin Res.
Unsan

NORTH KOREA
Hungnam

Sea of Japan

Pyongyang

Kimpo Airfield
Kaesong
38th parallel
Wolmi-do Island
Seoul
Inchon
Osan
Han R.
37th parallel

Taejon
R.

Yellow Sea

SOUTH KOREA
Naktong
No Name Ridge

JAPAN

Pusan

0   50   100 mi.
0 50 100 km

Itazuke AFB

As the NKPA closed in, Dean wanted to pull his men out of Taejon on July 18. General Walton H. Walker, the head of the 8th Army and commander of the ground forces in Korea, ordered him to hold the city for two more days.

25

U.S. artillery, such as the howitzer, played an important role in the battle against the armored forces of the NKPA.

Walker wanted to buy the time needed to deploy other American units that were arriving from Japan. During the two-day battle for Taejon, more than one quarter of the 4,000 U.S. soldiers defending the city were killed, wounded, or missing. Dean himself worked with small bazooka teams to hunt NKPA tanks. When his troops retreated from the city, Dean was separated from his men. He spent more than a month moving through enemy territory before he was captured by the NKPA. General Dean became the highest-ranking officer captured during the war. Dean was held as a prisoner of war until his release on September 4, 1953.

Taejon was another in a series of awful defeats for the U.S. troops. In a little more than two weeks, they had been pushed back 75 miles (120 km). Only five years earlier, at the end of World War II, the United States had one of the world's top military forces. Now its troops were being beaten by the better-trained and better-equipped forces of a smaller, poorer nation. The size of the U.S. military had shrunk from 15 million in 1945 to less than 2 million at the start of the Korean War. Political and military leaders in the United States believed that the greatest communist threat was in Europe. Because of this, the United States lacked proper defenses in the Far East.

"BUG OUT FEVER"

Panic among troops during wartime is common. In the early months of the Korean War, many U.N. troops were gripped by panic described as "bug out fever." Many frightened soldiers ran away rather than staying and fighting. They left behind their wounded comrades, their weapons, and anything else that might slow them down.

The U.N. forces were in retreat, but each day shiploads of troops arrived at the southern port city of Pusan to help even the score. The Korean War marked the first time that African-Americans fought in the same units as white soldiers. These arriving troops, black and white, quickly faced the brutal reality of the war. The United States had suffered more than 6,000 casualties in the first month alone.

Charles Rangel, now a U.S. congressman from New York who served in the U.S. Army during the Korean War, recalled:

> *We were greeted by trucks of dead GIs just stacked up like fireplace wood.*

27

General Walker moved all his forces back to set up a defensive line along the Naktong River in the southeastern corner of Korea. The Pusan Perimeter was about 100 miles (161 km) long and 50 miles (80 km) wide. It was the United Nations' last line of defense. If the NKPA broke through, U.N. forces would be pushed back to the Sea of Japan, and South Korea would be lost. In an inspiring message to his troops on July 29, 1950, Walker said that defeat was not an option:

> *There is no line behind us to which we can retreat. … We must fight until the end.*

British troops brought some much-needed relief to the weary American and South Korean troops in late August 1950.

In the intense summer heat, the NKPA launched attack after attack to try to break through the U.N. defenses. In mid-August, the North Koreans broke a hole in the line and crossed the Naktong River. Walker rushed in the Marines, who had recently arrived in Korea, to plug it up. The Marines fought

to recapture No Name Ridge, a 1½ mile (2.4-km) ridge that led directly south to Pusan. Losing it might have caused the Pusan Perimeter to fall apart.

On August 17, U.S. artillery pounded the hill. Marine Corsair fighter planes covered the area with bombs and machine-gun fire. The Marines began to climb the hill, taking fire from NKPA machine guns and mortars every step of the way. A *Time* magazine reporter who witnessed the Marines' heroism wrote:

Hell burst around [the Marines] as they moved up the barren face of the ridge. Everywhere along the assault line, men dropped. To continue looked impossible. But, all glory forever to the bravest men I ever saw, the line did not break. The casualties were unthinkable, but the assault force never turned back.

After two costly attempts, the Marines finally broke through and retook No Name Ridge.

The two sides waged similar bloody battles all along the line. The U.N. troops were now aided by the arrival of the first British troops and better weapons, including M-26 tanks. The NKPA could not break through the line. But U.S. military leaders realized they could never defeat their enemy by simply playing defense. General MacArthur had a bold plan that would help turn the tide. ◣

29

The Tide Turns at Inchon

Chapter

4

General MacArthur had been plotting an invasion behind North Korean lines since his brief visit to Korea in late June 1950. His plan was to land troops at Inchon, a port city on Korea's west coast about 20 miles (32 km) from Seoul. A successful landing would allow U.N. troops to move in behind the NKPA troops fighting in the Pusan region and cut off their supply routes.

It was a bold and dangerous plan. Many top U.S. military leaders met on August 23, 1950, to discuss the invasion. U.S. Navy Lieutenant Commander Arlie Capps told the group of U.S. officials:

> We drew up a list of every [possible] and natural handicap—and Inchon had 'em all.

Many high-ranking officers shared Capps' opinion. First of all, Inchon was protected by an island called Wolmi-do. Enemy forces there would have to be taken out before the invasion could take place. Another potential problem was that the channel that led to the port was extremely narrow. One disabled ship could block the advance of all those behind it.

However, the greatest concern was the extreme rise and fall of the tide. At low tide, the harbor turned to mud flats, which would have stranded the landing craft. The U.N. troops would have a window of only a few hours to secure Wolmi-do Island in the morning, and a few hours to unload troops in the evening. Once on the Inchon beach, troops would have to scale a 15-foot (4.5-meter) high sea wall. If the wall were heavily defended, the invading soldiers could easily be picked off.

MacArthur knew the dangers of landing at Inchon. He also believed that the NKPA knew it was a terrible place to launch an attack. As a result, MacArthur was confident that the enemy would have its guard down. After much debate, other military leaders finally agreed to the general's plan and held their breath.

MacArthur's invasion force included the 1st Marine Division. Many of these soldiers were battle-tested veterans who had fought bravely in World War II. The division also included Marines who had been defending the Pusan line.

General MacArthur (seated) watched the shelling of Inchon from the USS Mount McKinley.

MacArthur called the newly formed unit the X (Tenth) Corps. It consisted of more than 70,000 men, including the U.S. 7th Infantry Division and ROK marine units.

The invasion date was set for September 15, 1950. For two days prior, U.S. and British warships bombarded Wolmi-do Island and Inchon in the hope of weakening the enemy defenses in the landing areas. In the early morning hours of September 15, the landing craft carrying the first waves of Marines slipped into the water and moved toward Wolmi-do.

The naval bombing started once again. Marine Corsair planes hammered the island with one last round of bombs, rockets, and machine-gun fire. The first Marines stormed the island just after 6:30 A.M. They met little resistance and needed only a couple of hours to secure the island. They had taken more than 100 NKPA prisoners while suffering only 17 wounded and no deaths.

The main assault on Inchon could not begin until that evening because of the drastic tidal changes. Reports that the Wolmi-do landings had gone smoothly helped ease the soldiers' nerves as they waited in Inchon harbor. The deafening sound of bursting bombs and rockets from the U.N. warships and planes filled the air.

The guns suddenly went quiet at about 5:30 P.M., when the first waves of Marines dashed from their landing craft. The Marines used ladders to climb

AN INTERNATIONAL FIGHTING FORCE

Although the Korean War was a U.N. operation, the United States supplied about 90 percent of the men and war materials. Still, 16 other nations, including Turkey, the Philippines, Australia, Canada, and the United Kingdom, sent troops into the battle, and five others sent medical units. Other than the United States and the Republic of Korea, the United Kingdom suffered the most casualties: 1,000 dead, 2,500 wounded, and 1,000 missing in action.

U.S. Marines climbed ladders over the sea wall at Inchon on September 15, 1950.

the sea wall. On the other side, they found that many of the enemy trenches had been deserted. The Marines quickly moved inland and captured

key targets within the city of Inchon. By early morning on September 16, it was clear that MacArthur's risky plan had been a huge success. Roughly 13,000 Marines had made it ashore at a cost of fewer than 200 casualties, including only 21 dead.

As supplies, tanks, and other vehicles were moved ashore, MacArthur turned his attention toward recapturing Seoul. On September 17, the Marines captured Kimpo Airfield outside of the South Korean capital. During the next five days, more than 1,300 tons (1,170 metric tons) of U.N. supplies were flown in, and more than 300 wounded were flown out to hospitals in Japan. Kimpo quickly became the launching site for U.N. bombing missions over Seoul.

The NKPA was reeling, but its defenses stiffened around Seoul in late September. Marine Private Charlie Carmin described the street-fighting tactics used during the battle:

> *North Koreans had placed barricades across the street, made of large straw sacks filled with dirt. During the day, enemy rifle and automatic weapon fire from buildings lining the street covered these barricades, and it became very hazardous for a Marine to be seen moving on the street.*
>
> *The Marine solution was to clear each building one at a time as we leap-frogged forward. A rifleman's progress was slow, but the game was deadly if you screwed up.*

By September 28, the U.N. forces had reclaimed Seoul, much of which had been reduced to rubble.

To the South, General Walker's 8th Army had NKPA troops on the run. U.N. forces defending the Pusan region had launched a series of attacks that followed closely after the Inchon landing. As word of the defeat at Inchon spread, NKPA forces feared being surrounded and fled back toward the North.

An elderly man walked through a street in Seoul that was destroyed during the fighting between U.N. troops and the NKPA.

By the end of September, the goals set forth by the United Nations were met. Syngman Rhee's government had been restored in Seoul, and the NKPA had been pushed back over the 38th parallel. If the war had ended there, it would have been considered a major success. But the recent string of resounding victories prompted the United States to set a new goal: the elimination of communist troops in all of Korea. ◥

A New Enemy Emerges

MacArthur and other military leaders were convinced that a complete victory over communist forces was close at hand. South Korean President Syngman Rhee and the United Nations longed for a unified Korea with a democratic government. President Rhee urged the United States to cross the 38th parallel to wipe out the NKPA. The press, members of both political parties, and a large percentage of the American public also wanted total victory. President Truman agreed and gave MacArthur the go-ahead to cross the 38th parallel and reunify Korea.

However, Truman did not want the neighboring Chinese to view the invasion as a threat. As a precaution, only ROK troops would be allowed to advance into areas closest to the Chinese border.

Relations between the United States and China were unstable. Only a year before the fighting broke out in Korea, communist Chinese forces had won a long, bloody civil war. Led by Mao Tse-tung, the communists ousted the previous government and its leader, Chiang Kai-shek. The United States had supported Chiang Kai-shek's forces and continued to provide aid to them on Formosa (now called Taiwan). China's communist government worried that if the United States took over all of Korea, an invasion of China might be next.

McCarthy's Influence

During the Korean War, the United States was in the midst of an anti-communism campaign led by Senator Joseph McCarthy. Among other things, the senator claimed that "reds," or communists, in Truman's government had allowed China to fall to Mao Tse-tung's communist forces. Such claims were untrue, but they had a tremendous effect on the American public. The "Red Scare," as it became known, fueled the public's desire to see the communists defeated in Korea.

Mao Tse-tung officially declared the founding of the People's Republic of China on October 1, 1949.

On October 1, 1950, President Rhee sent the first ROK troops across the 38th parallel. Eight days later, the first U.S. troops followed them across the border into North Korea. MacArthur's strategy for the invasion of North Korea included the first in a string of major mistakes: With the NKPA clearly on the run, he decided to divide his forces.

General Walker's 8th Army would move up the west coast from Seoul to the North Korean capital of Pyongyang. Meanwhile, X Corps soldiers were sent on boats around the Korean peninsula to the east coast. The move wasted time and kept some of the top U.S. troops—who had fought so well at Inchon and Seoul—out of action during a crucial time.

Despite this, the 8th Army steamed ahead and captured Pyongyang on October 19, 1950. By this time, the NKPA was a broken force. Most of its large weapons and tanks had been left behind during its retreat from the South.

On October 15, President Truman and General MacArthur had flown to Wake Island, a small, U.S.-held territory in the Pacific, to discuss what they thought would be the final phase of the war. It was the first time the two men had met.

Truman's main concern was the possible entry of China into the war. MacArthur, confident as always, told the president that the Chinese were no longer a threat. If Chinese troops did join the fighting, MacArthur vowed to destroy them.

What MacArthur and Truman did not know was that thousands of Chinese troops had already begun to move secretly into Korea. By the end of October, more than 300,000 Chinese troops had slipped across the Yalu River and into North Korea.

President Harry Truman presented General MacArthur with the Medal of Merit during a brief conference on Wake Island.

Soldiers from X Corps hit the beach at Wonson on the east coast of North Korea in October 1950. Within weeks, they would be fighting thousands of Chinese troops.

Chinese troops nearly wiped out ROK troops in a series of small battles in late October, but MacArthur dismissed them as small, unorganized groups of volunteers. In fact, the invaders were battle-proven members of the Chinese People's Liberation Army.

The Chinese removed any doubt about their presence when they attacked the U.S. 8th Cavalry Regiment on November 1, 1950. About 20,000 Chinese troops surprised the regiment near Unsan, 80 miles (128 km) north of Pyongyang.

The Americans were confused by sounds they had never heard on the battlefield: shrill whistles and the eerie wail of bugles. The Chinese used these instruments in place of radios to coordinate their attacks. They were sounds that U.S. troops in Korea would soon learn to fear.

The soldiers of the 8th Cavalry watched in horror as a sea of Chinese troops moved toward them. The Chinese launched wild charges directly into enemy gunfire. But the sheer size of the Chinese force allowed them to slice into the U.S. lines. This type of attack, known as a human wave assault, would become all too familiar to U.N. and U.S. troops over the coming months.

Fierce hand-to-hand fighting broke out, as the Americans fought in vain to repel the bayonet charges of their attackers. The Americans went into full retreat, suffering heavy losses along the way. The Chinese struck the U.N. lines again the following night. Sleeping troops awoke to sounds of Chinese bugles. Lieutenant W.C. Hill described what happened next:

> *Then, as though they came out of a burst of smoke, shadowy figures started shooting and bayoneting everybody they could find.*

43

U.S. soldiers braved harsh weather to attend a religious service on Thanksgiving Day in 1950.

44

One battalion of the 8th Cavalry was hit especially hard. They fought bravely for several days, but they were simply no match for the much larger force of enemy troops. In the end, more than 600 of the 800-man American unit were dead or captured.

The Chinese made similar savage attacks on American positions over the next few days. They struck at night and then quickly retreated before the dazed U.N. and ROK forces knew what had hit them.

Then a strange thing happened: The Chinese assaults suddenly stopped. MacArthur mistook this as a sign that the Chinese were in retreat. In fact, they were preparing for one of their biggest attacks yet.

Meanwhile, MacArthur was planning a new offensive that he hoped would win the war. However, his commanders privately worried about sending their men back into an area where they had recently been defeated. Still, MacArthur confidently told reporters that if all went well, American troops would be home by Christmas.

On November 23, 1950, the troops celebrated Thanksgiving with a hot turkey dinner. The following morning, they would begin a march toward disaster. ◣

THE FIRST JET FIGHTERS

Clashes with the Chinese extended to the skies. The war in Korea marked the first time that the United States used jet fighters in combat. On November 8, 1950, a U.S. Air Force F-80 jet fighter piloted by Lieutenant Russell Brown shot down a Soviet-built MiG-15 near the Yalu River. It was the first-ever aerial dogfight between two jets.

Winter Woes

Chapter

6

On the morning of November 24, 1950, General Walton Walker's 8th Army began to rumble forward again. They moved without meeting any large pockets of enemy troops until the following night. Whistle blasts and bugle calls once again filled the night air. The Chinese launched their largest human wave assault yet, plowing into the U.N. and ROK troops with a force of more than 100,000 men. The overwhelmed U.N. troops had no choice but to fall back.

By this time, U.N. troops also had to contend with another enemy: the harsh winter weather that swept across the Korean peninsula. It was the coldest winter in 100 years, with temperatures regularly dipping below freezing. Captain Sherman Pratt recalled how the

In November 1950, ROK and U.N. troops continued to clash with Chinese soldiers. Meanwhile, people in Seoul tried to salvage anything they could from the ruins of the shattered city.

Halted in their tracks by a Chinese roadblock, U.S. and U.N. troops tried to stay warm in subzero temperatures.

painfully cold weather added to the misery of the retreating troops:

> *It dulled our senses. It made us move slow. It made us think slow. Wounded men who otherwise might have survived died because they couldn't be kept warm. Our vehicles*

wouldn't start. Batteries gave out. The grease on our rifles turned to glue and they wouldn't fire. Our rations would freeze solid. Men would carry cans of food around inside their clothes, under their armpits, trying to thaw them a little so they could be eaten.

To make matters worse, the enemy did not appear to be bothered by the cold. Chinese troops moved along the snow-covered ground in canvas tennis shoes. Stunned American soldiers even told stories of finding dead Chinese soldiers who had fought in bare feet.

Two days after striking the 8th Army on the west coast, the Chinese zeroed in on the men of X Corps, whom MacArthur had sent to the other side of the country. A swarm of 120,000 attackers pinned down the outnumbered U.S. troops along the Chosin Reservoir, a huge man-made lake that supplied hydroelectric power to the region.

The 1st Marine Division was cut off and nearly surrounded. Their only chance of survival was to march 55 miles (88 km) to the port city of Hungnam. When asked about his division's retreat, General Oliver Smith replied:

We're not retreating. We're just advancing in another direction.

Smith's famous response highlighted the fighting spirit of his men, who would have to battle the Chinese and the weather almost every step of the way.

A 240-man unit led by Captain William Barber was assigned to defend a hill overlooking Toktong Pass, an escape route for the two Marine regiments in the area. At about 1:30 A.M. on November 28, the Chinese attacked. As the fighting began, Private Hector Cafferata jumped out of his sleeping bag and began firing at enemy soldiers only 30 feet (9 m) away. He recalled:

> *I fought all night in socks and no parka. I didn't have time to get dressed. There was about six inches of snow and it was about thirty degrees below zero. My feet felt like two blocks of ice.*

Cafferata held his M-1 rifle in one hand and a small shovel he used to swat away enemy grenades in the other. He continued fighting until well after dawn. He and the other brave Marines had driven the Chinese back.

Though he was advised to withdraw, Captain Barber refused to leave until the last group of Marines made it safely through the pass. Later, he and Cafferata both received Medals of Honor for their courage. They were only two of the many heroes who emerged during the battle of the "Frozen Chosin."

Soldiers from the 1st Marine Division helped two Marine regiments safely withdraw from the Chosin Reservoir area.

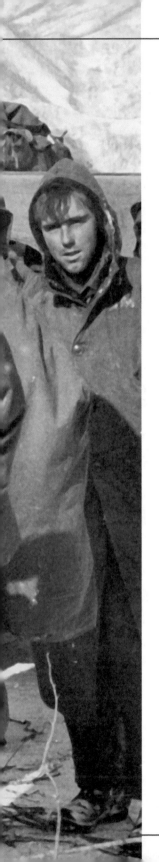

For two weeks, the men of X Corps marched across the mountainous terrain. Stopping was not an option for the exhausted troops. If the Chinese did not get them, the cold weather would. During the long march, relief came from above. Bombs and machine-gun fire from U.S. fighter-bombers kept the road to Hungnam clear. Transport aircraft dropped in much-needed supplies.

By mid-December 1950, U.S. Navy ships had evacuated more than 105,000 U.S. and ROK troops and 91,000 Korean refugees from Hungnam. More than 17,000 vehicles and 300,000 tons (270,000 metric tons) of supplies had also been saved.

The escape from the Chosin Reservoir was an amazing feat, but it was hardly the total victory that MacArthur had predicted only weeks before.

By December 13, the battle-weary 8th Army had withdrawn all the way back below the 38th parallel. Their massive retreat was surpassed only by that of North Korean civilians. With their homeland in ruins, North Korean refugees poured into South Korea in search of a better way of life.

Soldiers from X Corps awaited supply drops during the march out of the "Frozen Chosin."

53

Thousands of North Korean refugees fled from Pyongyang by crossing the icy waters of the Taedong River to escape from the approaching Chinese army. The refugees slowly made their way to South Korea.

Eight-year-old TaeIm Park was one of the countless thousands who crossed the border. In December 1950, TaeIm, her 5-year-old brother JaeJun, her mother, her grandparents, and her aunt and uncle left Pyongyang on a 100-mile (161-km) trek south. During the month-long walk, TaeIm and her family braved the harsh weather. When warplanes flew overhead, her grandfather would yell for everyone to hug a tree, and the family would scramble for cover.

After crossing the 38th parallel, TaeIm's family followed the frozen Han River into Yongdungpo,

54

a town just outside of Seoul. From there, they traveled on top of a railroad car into the South Korean capital. TaeIm's grandfather tied everyone in the family together with sheets so that none of them would fall off. TaeIm's family eventually started a new life in Seoul. Their story is typical of the struggles faced by Korean refugees throughout the war.

Meanwhile, the shell-shocked U.N. troops had their own challenges to face. Any hopes of being home by Christmas were long gone. On December 23, the troops received more bad news. A jeep carrying General Walker ran head-on into a ROK army truck and was thrown into a ditch. The man who had led the U.N. troops so bravely at Pusan was dead.

No Substitute for Victory

After General Walker's death, General Matthew Ridgway was called in to replace him. Ridgway was a highly respected leader who had led the famed 82nd Airborne Division during World War II. In Korea, he inherited a fighting force that was low on morale. He observed:

> *It was clear to me that our troops had lost confidence. I could read it in their eyes, in their walk. I could read it in the faces of their leaders.*

It was easy to understand why the troops lacked fighting spirit. For the last month, they had been steadily beaten back by the Chinese forces. In early January 1951, the Chinese captured Seoul and then Inchon. By January 15, they had pushed U.N. troops south of the 37th

Chinese communist troops marched into South Korea to recapture Seoul.

parallel. In the six months since U.N. troops first entered the war, they had gained little—except mounting casualties.

Ridgway's plan for restoring his men's confidence included replacing many top commanders. He replaced officers who were too old or too inexperienced with younger men who had proven themselves in combat. He also changed the overall battlefield strategy. He wanted his troops to depend less on roads and focus instead on the high ground, where Chinese forces were usually lurking.

Ridgway also believed that the superior U.N. artillery force had not been used to its full advantage. If used properly, U.N. firepower could mow down the Chinese assaults and limit the number of U.N. casualties.

At the end of January, Ridgway launched a new offensive. Soldiers who had grown used to retreating began to take back much of the land they had lost over the past month. Morale among men in the field soared.

By this time, the Chinese troops were in bad shape. The harsh winter caused the same problems for them as it did for U.N. soldiers, including frozen weapons and frostbite. The deeper they moved into South Korea, the longer their supply routes grew.

Unlike the U.N. forces, the Chinese did not have the benefit of planes and trucks to deliver food, ammunition, and medical supplies. Most of their supplies were carried on foot or on mules. As a result, troops often did not have enough to eat or drink. Many went into combat unarmed and picked up the rifles of their dead or wounded comrades.

Winter camouflage suits worn by U.N. troops kept them warmer than their communist foes

59

Thousands had been killed or wounded in the human wave assaults of the past two months. Also, because the Chinese had poor front-line medical care, many wounded soldiers were simply left on the battlefield to die.

Meanwhile, U.N. casualties received the finest care available. The Korean War marked the first time that mobile army surgical hospitals, or MASH units, were used in combat. Helicopters airlifted wounded soldiers to these hospitals, which were

The ability to get immediate medical attention to wounded men helped save the lives of thousands of U.N. soldiers during the Korean War.

61

located close to the front lines. MASH surgeons often worked around the clock. The heavy volume of casualties forced the doctors to make tough decisions. In his famous book *MASH*, U.S. Army surgeon Richard Hooker recalled:

> *Sometimes we deliberately sacrifice a leg to save a life. ... We may lose a leg because if we spent an extra hour trying to save it another guy ... could die from being operated on too late.*

These MASH units played a vital role in the war effort by saving thousands of lives and enabling countless troops to return to the battlefield.

On March 15, 1951, the Chinese abandoned Seoul—the fourth and last time the South Korean capital changed hands. Within days, U.N. troops once again closed in on the 38th parallel.

Plotting the next step in the war became a great debate. By this time, many leaders, including President Truman, realized that the war to take all of Korea could not be won. As troops inched toward South Korea's original border, Truman saw an opportunity to begin peace talks. This angered MacArthur, who still wanted a complete victory.

Tensions between MacArthur and Truman had been growing for some time. For months, MacArthur had publicly protested Truman's "limited war." The general repeatedly demanded that the U.S. Army be allowed to bomb China. This strategy worried Truman, who feared that an action against China itself might bring the Soviet Union into the war. MacArthur also wanted the former Chinese leader Chiang Kai-shek's Chinese nationalist troops to join the war on the United Nations' side. But Truman believed this would only strengthen the resolve of Mao Tse-tung's communist forces and prolong the war.

The United Nations continued to drop supplies and paratroopers behind enemy lines, as President Truman searched for a way to a peace settlement.

On March 20, Truman issued a draft of a cease-fire plan that would be sent to China. After reading the proposal, MacArthur issued his own statement without informing any of his bosses back in Washington, D.C. In the statement, MacArthur threatened to expand the war beyond Korean borders if the Chinese did not give up.

Truman was furious. MacArthur did not have the authority to issue such a threat. The general

Chiang Kai-shek regularly inspected his troops on the Tachen Islands, off the coast of China. General MacArthur wanted to use Chiang Kai-shek's soldiers to fight Chinese troops, but President Truman refused.

had also destroyed any chance of a quick peace agreement.

The feud between Truman and MacArthur reached its boiling point on April 5, 1951. In a letter that was read before the U.S. Congress, MacArthur again called for the use of Chiang Kai-shek's troops in Korea. He also attacked Truman's policy in Korea by writing:

There is no substitute for victory.

65

After being removed from his post by President Truman, General MacArthur was given a grand homecoming in several American cities, including a huge ticker-tape parade in New York City.

The president viewed this as a direct and very public challenge to his authority. He would not tolerate MacArthur's antics any longer. On April 11, 1951, Truman relieved MacArthur of his command in Korea.

MacArthur came home to a hero's welcome. Despite his blunders in Korea, many Americans still saw him as the brilliant leader who had helped defeat the Japanese in World War II only six years earlier. Thousands of supporters turned up to greet him in Honolulu and San Francisco.

On April 19, record numbers of Americans tuned in their radios and televisions to hear the general make his farewell speech to Congress. MacArthur closed the speech with these famous words:

> *I still remember the refrain of one the most popular barracks ballads [of my early days in the military], which proclaimed most proudly that old soldiers never die; they just fade away. And like the old soldier of that ballad, I now close my military career and just fade away, an old soldier who tried to do his duty as God gave him the light to see that duty. Goodbye.*

Tremendous applause swept through the hall. Three days later, MacArthur's farewell tour ended with a ticker-tape parade through New York City. The general was showered with a blizzard of paper by more than 7 million people who turned out to honor him.

Meanwhile, dismissing MacArthur hurt the president's already declining popularity. A national poll in mid-March showed that Truman's approval rating was only 26 percent. Most Americans had supported the war at first, believing that the United States would quickly stomp out the communist threat. But as the war dragged on, and thousands of troops died, public opinion changed. Most Americans were no longer interested in supporting a war that could not be won.

Tanks and other vehicles provided an advantage for U.N. troops over Chinese soldiers as the fighting continued in 1951.

Back in Korea, General Ridgway assumed MacArthur's post as supreme commander of the U.N. forces. General James Van Fleet took over Ridgway's previous role as commander of all ground troops. The seesaw battle between the U.N. and Chinese forces continued through the spring. The Chinese launched major offensives in late April and again in May. Both times, U.N. forces were pushed back for a short time, only to regain the ground they had lost. Superior U.N. artillery and airpower inflicted shocking numbers of casualties on enemy troops.

By the end of June, the jagged U.N. line extended as far as 40 miles (64 km) north of the 38th parallel and several miles below it on Korea's west coast. The boundaries were not much different than they had been when the fighting started a year before. But the cost had been great. Casualty figures on both sides reached into the hundreds of thousands. This included American losses of more than 21,000 dead and 78,000 wounded or captured. ◣

A Forgotten War

The first big step toward peace in Korea came from an unlikely source. In a radio broadcast on June 23, 1951, the Soviet Union's U.N. Ambassador Jacob Malik discussed a possible cease-fire and the withdrawal of foreign troops from Korea. Malik had returned to the United Nations after the Soviet Union's boycott of the U.N. Security Council ended. The Chinese and North Koreans agreed with the plan their communist allies in the Soviet Union proposed. Both nations had suffered huge losses of men and territory. Within a week, General Ridgway officially invited the leaders of the Chinese and North Korean forces to sit down to discuss a peace agreement.

On July 10, the two sides met for the first time at Kaesong. The ancient city on Korea's west coast stood on the southern tip of the area held

by the communists. The talks moved along slowly. Neither side wanted to give in to the other's demands. The main issue was where to draw the line that divided North and South Korea. The Chinese and North Koreans wanted the border restored at the 38th parallel. The United Nations wanted to keep the existing lines, which would expand the size of South Korea. Both sides refused to budge, and the talks broke off on August 23.

As the peace process ground to a halt, bloody battles between U.N. and communist forces raged on. But neither side was willing to risk the huge casualties that went along with launching a major attack. Instead, the war in Korea became a struggle for the high ground.

Communist delegates left the peace talks at Kaesong in July 1951. The talks broke off a month later after the two sides could not agree upon the dividing line between North and South Korea.

In mid-September, U.N. forces began their assault on a 4 mile (6 km) line of rugged peaks known as Heartbreak Ridge. NKPA soldiers in deep bunkers rained gunfire, grenades, and mortars down on the U.N. troops who fought their way up the steep terrain. U.S. Colonel James Adams said:

Soldiers fought in cities and on mountain ranges toward the end of the Korean War.

> *We've tried every approach to that mountain. We've crawled up every finger of the ridge. That's right—crawled. You can't climb up it. It's like a razor.*

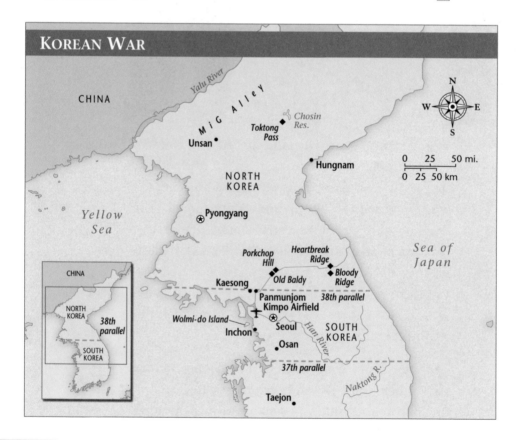

KOREAN WAR

U.N. troops finally took control of the ridge on October 15. Victory came at a heavy price, though, as casualties of U.S. and U.N. troops numbered 3,700.

A U.S. soldier wounded in fighting on Pork Chop Hill was carried off by fellow troops.

For the remainder of the war, U.N. troops adapted to living and fighting in the hills. The only way for soldiers to get food, water, and ammunition was to lug it up the hills themselves. Days of furious fighting were followed by long periods of boredom and uncertainty.

Troops on both sides spent much of the time digging trenches, filling sandbags, and building bunkers. Intense clashes on the slopes of hills such as Old Baldy, Bloody Ridge, and Pork Chop Hill took on the look of the trench warfare of World War I. Most of these hills were not even of great military importance. But each small victory could be used as a bargaining chip during future peace talks.

Talks started up again on October 25 at Panmunjom on the northwestern border of the territory controlled by the United Nations. The communists finally relented and agreed to accept the existing battle lines as the permanent Korean border. A month into the meetings, peace seemed to be close at hand.

However, the two sides could not come to an agreement about the release of prisoners of war (POWs). The communists wanted all of the nearly

170,000 POWs held by the United Nations returned to them. This included more than 16,000 South Korean troops who had been captured and forced to serve in the NKPA. The United Nations also claimed that thousands more Chinese and North Korean POWs wanted to stay in South Korea. President Truman argued that forcing these troops to return home would be a death sentence. Neither side would give in. This single issue would prolong the war for more than 18 months.

Negotiators representing the United Nations and North Korea discussed the boundaries of North and South Korea during the peace talks at Panmunjom.

75

In an effort to speed along the peace process, the United Nations stepped up the air war in North Korea. The plan was to cripple the North Korean economy by taking out key industrial targets. In late June 1952, American fighter-bombers struck North Korea's hydroelectric dams. This knocked out much of the country's power supply. It was just another example of the aerial advantage held by the U.N. forces.

Since the war's early days, U.S. pilots had ruled the skies over Korea. B-26 and giant B-29 bombers pounded bridges, airfields, and other strategic targets in North Korea. Fighter-bombers destroyed railroads and supply convoys. Over South Korea, U.S. Air Force, Navy, and Marine fighter-bombers attacked the swarms of North Korean and Chinese soldiers. Without air support, U.S. and U.N. foot soldiers would not have stood a chance against the much larger communist forces.

The superior skill of U.S. pilots was on display in the area just south of the Yalu River known as MiG Alley. There, U.S. F-86 Sabrejets tangled with Soviet-built MiG-15 jets. Though usually

FAMOUS KOREAN WAR PILOTS

The list of American pilots that flew during the Korean War includes some famous names. Ted Williams and John Glenn often flew missions together in Marine F9F jets. At the time, Williams was already an all-star slugger for the Boston Red Sox. Glenn later became the first American astronaut to orbit Earth. The first two men to walk on the moon also saw combat in Korea. Edwin "Buzz" Aldrin shot down two MiGs in an F-86, and Neil Armstrong flew 78 missions for the U.S. Navy.

outnumbered, the well-trained U.S. pilots shot down enemy fighters at a rate of 10 to one. Pilots who shot down at least five enemy planes were called "aces." In Korea, 40 American pilots became aces.

U.S. and U.N. aircrews were vital in carrying out bombing and attack missions in the Korean War.

Despite the victories in the sky, the United Nations was not getting any closer to a peace settlement. Back in the United States, Korea became the key issue in the 1952 presidential election. Before the war even started, President Truman had decided that he would not seek another term. In November 1952, Dwight D. Eisenhower ran against Adlai Stevenson and

defeated him in a landslide. Eisenhower was a popular U.S. Army general who had commanded the invasion force on D-Day during World War II. Americans believed he was the right man to bring about a quick end to the war in Korea.

But Eisenhower was not the new leader who would play the biggest role in ending the war. On March 5, 1953, Russian leader Josef Stalin died.

Dwight Eisenhower (center), who had been recently elected president, fulfilled a campaign promise by visiting American troops in Korea in December 1952. He visited with soldiers from the 3rd Infantry Division, the unit he commanded during World War II.

American leaders had long suspected that Stalin held up the peace process in Korea. They believed he wished to keep the United States away from focusing on Europe for as long as possible. These suspicions seemed to hold true when Stalin's successor, Georgi Malenkov, talked of settling disputes with the United States less than two weeks after he took office.

BRAINWASHING

The communists tried to break the spirits of many POWs by denying them food and constantly harassing them. As part of their daily routine, POWs were forced to listen to hours of lectures meant to convert them to communism. This type of physical and mental torture became known as "brainwashing."

The North Koreans and Chinese followed the Soviet Union's lead. In late March 1953, the communists agreed to an exchange of sick and wounded prisoners. The transfer of prisoners, called Operation Little Switch, began on April 20. The communists released 684 U.N. prisoners, including 149 Americans, in exchange for more than 7,000 of their own men.

The poor physical condition of the returned U.N. soldiers was shocking. After months of neglect and brutality at the hands of their captors, many of the men were barely alive. Thousands of prisoners of war had died of starvation and dysentery. Corporal Eugene Inman of the U.S. Army spent 33 months in communist prison camps. After being captured in late November 1950, he was forced to march 500 miles (800 km) to a camp that prisoners called Death Valley. Inman described life in the camp:

> *It was eight months following my capture before I was permitted to remove my clothes. When I did, they were alive with lice. We slept literally jammed into a tiny room. We worked out a schedule, sleeping first on the left sides, then on our right sides. There wasn't room for anybody to lie flat on his back.*

U.S. prisoners of war had to deal with poor treatment and horrible prison conditions during the Korean War.

Operation Little Switch was a huge step toward finally bringing an end to the war. But as the two sides moved closer to a peace agreement, South Korean President Syngman Rhee almost destroyed the whole plan. From the beginning, he wanted no part in the peace talks. He also vowed never to sign a truce that did not reunite his homeland.

On June 18, Rhee ordered ROK guards at South Korean prison camps to release all prisoners who did not want to return to their communist homeland. More than 25,000 troops were freed into the streets of South Korea. U.N. leaders feared Rhee's action would cause the communists to break off the talks, and they quickly issued an apology.

Despite this setback, on July 27, 1953, U.N. and communist representatives signed an armistice at Panmunjom. Faced with the threat of losing all American military and economic aid, Rhee had no choice but to give in. He would not sign the armistice, but he agreed to follow its terms. At 10 P.M., the battlefield fell silent.

The large-scale exchange of prisoners, called Operation Big Switch, began in August. The United Nations returned more than 70,000 North Koreans and 6,000 Chinese prisoners. Nearly 13,000 U.N. prisoners, including 3,597 Americans, were free once again.

After nearly three years of fighting, very little had changed. Korea remained divided into two separate nations. The borders were not much different than they had been at the start of the war.

For the people of Korea, the war never officially ended because President Rhee refused to sign the peace agreement.

British POWs sailed to England after Operation

Today, more than 50 years after the end of the war, tensions still exist along the demilitarized zone (DMZ), the 2½ mile (4-km) wide area that separates the two countries. The United States continues to play a role in keeping the peace, with thousands of troops stationed throughout South Korea.

The Korean War Veterans Memorial in Washington, D.C., was dedicated in 1995 to honor the soldiers who served to protect South Korea from North Korea's invasion.

The Korean War is often referred to as the forgotten war. During the last two years of the war, much of the news out of Korea focused on stalled peace talks or needless deaths in unnecessary battles. The American public seemed to have simply lost interest.

Even today, the Korean War is overshadowed by the historic victory in World War II and the controversy of the Vietnam War. Many Americans are not familiar with the important battles or even the goals of the war in Korea.

What is often lost in discussions about the war is that the United Nations actually achieved one of its original goals. For the first time, free nations banded together to repel an invading force.

The Korean War may not be as well-known as other struggles, but the sacrifices made by the men and women who fought and served in the war are certainly no less. They gave their lives to protect people they did not know in a land many of them had never heard of. ◣

Timeline

1910

Korea becomes a colony of Japan

August 6, 1945

The United States drops an atomic bomb on Hiroshima, Japan

August 8, 1945

The Soviet Union declares war on Japan

August 11, 1945

Korea is divided into Soviet and U.S. zones along the 38th parallel

September 2, 1945

Soviet troops stop their advance into Korea at the 38th parallel; the Japanese formally surrender aboard the USS *Missouri*; World War II ends

September 8, 1945

U.S. troops arrive in Korea to accept the Japanese surrender

August 15, 1948

The Republic of Korea officially forms in the area we call South Korea; Syngman Rhee becomes the country's first president

September 9, 1948

North Korea is renamed the Democratic People's Republic of Korea; Kim Il Sung becomes its premier

June 29, 1949

The last U.S. combat troops leave South Korea; several hundred military advisers are left behind

October 1, 1949

Mao Tse-tung forms the People's Republic of China

June 25, 1950

North Korean troops cross the 38th parallel to invade South Korea; South Korean troops advance to the front lines

June 27, 1950

President Truman approves the use of the U.S. Air Force and Navy to aid South Korea

June 28, 1950

Seoul, the South Korean capital, falls to troops from North Korea

June 29, 1950

General Douglas MacArthur flies from Japan to Korea to observe the fighting

June 30, 1950

President Truman grants General MacArthur's request to send U.S. ground forces to Korea

July 5, 1950

Task Force Smith is defeated by North Korean troops, north of Osan

July 29, 1950

General Walton Walker orders U.N. troops along the Pusan Perimeter to "stand or die"

September 15, 1950

 U.N. forces land at Inchon

September 28, 1950

U.N. troops are in control of Seoul

October 1, 1950

South Korean troops cross the 38th parallel into North Korea

October 9, 1950

U.S. troops cross the 38th parallel and enter North Korea for the first time

October 15, 1950

 At a meeting on Wake Island, General MacArthur assures President Truman that the Chinese are not a threat

October 19, 1950

U.N. forces capture Pyongyang, the North Korean capital

November 1, 1950

 U.S. troops clash with large numbers of Chinese soldiers for the first time, near the city of Unsan

November 27–December 14, 1950

U.N. troops withdraw from the Chosin Reservoir to the port in Hungnam

December 23, 1950

General Walton Walker is killed in an accident; General Matthew Ridgway takes over command of ground forces in Korea

January 5, 1951

 Chinese troops take control of Seoul

March 18, 1951

Seoul is recaptured for the final time by U.N. troops

April 11, 1951

Truman relieves General MacArthur of his command

Timeline

April 19, 1951

General MacArthur gives his famous farewell speech to Congress; he had been given a hero's welcome upon his return to the United States

June 23, 1951

Soviet Ambassador Jacob Malik urges a cease-fire and peace talks in Korea

July 10, 1951

Peace talks begin at Kaesong, but the fighting continues

August 23, 1951

The talks come to a halt

October 15, 1951

After more than a month of bloody battles, U.N. troops capture Heartbreak Ridge

October 25, 1951

Peace talks resume at Panmunjom

November 4, 1952

Dwight Eisenhower is elected U.S. president

December 5–8, 1952

Eisenhower fulfills a campaign promise by visiting troops in Korea

March 5, 1953

Soviet Premier Josef Stalin dies

April 20, 1953

Operation Little Switch, the first exchange of prisoners of war, begins

July 27, 1953

U.N. and communist representatives sign an armistice; the fighting in Korea ends

August 5, 1953

Operation Big Switch, the second exchange of prisoners of war, begins

On The Web

For more information on *The Korean War*, use FactHound.

1 Go to *www.facthound.com*

2 Type in a search word related to this book or this book ID: 0756516250

3 Click on the *Fetch It* button. FactHound will find Web sites related to this book

Historic Sites

Korean War Veterans National Museum and Library
1007 Pacesetter Drive
Rantoul, IL 61866
217/893-4111

Books and manuscripts, maps and photographs, and military and civilian documents associated with the Korean War

Korean War Veterans Memorial
900 Ohio Drive S.W.
Washington, DC 20024
202/426-6841

Sculptures and a memorial dedicated to those soldiers who fought bravely in the Korean War

Look for all the books in this series

The Cuban Missile Crisis:
To the Brink of War
ISBN 0-7565-1624-2

Hiroshima and Nagasaki:
Fire from the Sky
ISBN 0-7565-1621-8

The Korean War:
America's Forgotten War
ISBN 0-7565-1625-0

Pearl Harbor:
Day of Infamy
ISBN 0-7565-1622-6

September 11:
Attack on America
ISBN 0-7565-1620-X

The Tet Offensive:
Turning Point of the Vietnam War
ISBN 0-7565-1623-4

Glossary

ambassador

a government official who represents his or her country in a foreign country

armistice

a formal agreement to end the fighting during a war

artillery

powerful weapons, such as cannons, howitzers, and missile launchers, that fire rockets or shells

battalion

a U.S. military group made up of four to six to companies of soldiers; a battalion can include up to 1,000 troops

bayonet

a blade attached the end of a rifle and used as a weapon in close combat

C ration

short for combat ration, the packaged meals soldiers ate during World War II, Korea, and Vietnam

cavalry

a highly mobile army unit that relies on light armor transportation and helicopters

communism

a political system in which there is no private property and everything is owned and shared in common

company

a U.S. military group made up of three to five platoons of soldiers

corps

a large U.S. military group made up of two to five divisions of soldiers; a corps can include more than 40,000 troops

division

a large U.S. military group made up of three regiments (or brigades) of soldiers; a division can include as many as 15,000 troops

dysentery

a disease of the intestines often caused by a lack of proper food and water

infantry

the branch of an army made up of units trained to fight on foot

platoon

a U.S. military group made up of two to four squads of soldiers

regiment

a U.S. military group made up of two to five battalions of soldiers; also known as a brigade

squad

about 12 infantry soldiers in an army

Source Notes

Chapter 1

Page 8, line 13: David McCullough. *Truman*. New York: Simon & Schuster, 1992, p. 775.

Chapter 3

Page 20, line 11: Joseph C. Goulden. *Korea: The Untold Story of the War*. New York: McGraw-Hill Book Company, 1982, p. 53.

Page 24, line 3: Rudy Tomedi. *No Bugles, No Drums: An Oral History of the Korean War*. New York: John Wiley & Sons, Inc., 1994, p. 4.

Page 27, line 31: *Korean War Stories*. PBS Home Video, 2001.

Page 28, line 11: Roy E. Appleman. *South to the Naktong, North to the Yalu*. Washington, D.C.: Office of the Chief of Military History, 1961, p. 208.

Page 29, line 12: James Bell. "The Battle of No Name Ridge." *Time*. 28 Aug. 1950.

Chapter 4

Page 30, line 15: *Korea: The Untold Story of the War*, p. 193.

Page 35, line 21: Charlie Carmin. "Veterans' Memoirs." *Korean War Educator*. 23 Nov. 2005 <http://www.koreanwar-educator.org/memoirs/carmin/#seoul>

Chapter 5

Page 43, line 28: "Crazy Horse Rides Again." *Time*. 13 Nov. 1950.

SOURCE NOTES

Chapter 6

Page 48, line 3: *No Bugles, No Drums: An Oral History of the Korean War*, p. 68.

Page 49, line 25: "Retreat of the 20,000." *Time.* 18 Dec. 1950.

Page 50, line 9: Larry Smith. *Beyond Glory: Medal of Honor Winners in Their Own Words*. New York: W.W. Norton & Company, 2003, p. 136.

Chapter 7

Page 56, line 8: Matthew B. Ridgway. *Soldier*. New York: Harper & Brothers, 1956, p. 204.

Page 62, line 6: Richard Hooker. *MASH*. Mattituck, N.Y.: Rivercity Press, 1976, p. 160.

Page 65, line 9: Douglas MacArthur. *Reminiscences*. New York: McGraw-Hill Book Company, 1964, p. 386.

Page 67, line 7: "The Old Soldier." *Time.* 30 April 1951.

Chapter 8

Page 72, line 8: "The Dim-Out War." *Time.* 8 Oct. 1951.

Page 81, line 3: Harry Spiller, ed. *American POWs in Korea: Sixteen Personal Accounts*. Jefferson, N.C.: McFarland & Company, Inc., Publishers, 1998, p. 87.

SELECT BIBLIOGRAPHY

Blair, Clay. *The Forgotten War*. New York: Doubleday, 1987.

Goulden, Joseph C. *Korea: The Untold Story of the War*. New York: McGraw-Hill Book Company, 1982.

Isserman, Maurice. *America at War: Korean War*. New York: Facts on File, Inc., 2003.

Lawson, Don. *The United States in the Korean War: Defending Freedom's Frontier*. New York: Abelard-Schuman, 1964.

MacArthur, Douglas. *Reminiscences*. New York: McGraw-Hill Book Company, 1964.

McCullough, David. *Truman*. New York: Simon & Schuster, 1992.

Smith, Larry. *Beyond Glory: Medal of Honor Winners in Their Own Words*. New York: W.W. Norton & Company, 2003.

Spiller, Harry, ed. *American POWs in Korea: Sixteen Personal Accounts*. Jefferson, N.C.: McFarland & Company, Inc., Publishers, 1998.

FURTHER READING

Ashabranner, Brent. *The Korean War Veterans Memorial: Remembering Korea*. Brookfield, Conn.: Twenty-First Century Books, 2001.

Fox, Mary Virginia. *The Importance of Douglas MacArthur*. San Diego: Lucent Books, 1999.

Lazo, Caroline Evensen. *Presidential Leaders: Harry S. Truman*. Minneapolis: Lerner Publications Company, 2003.

Uschan, Michael V. *The Korean War*. San Diego: Lucent Books, 2001.

Index

ABOUT THE AUTHOR

Brian Fitzgerald has worked in children's publishing for more than a decade. During that time, he has written about many of the key people and most important events in American history and popular culture—from World War II to Jimi Hendrix. He lives in Stamford, Connecticut.

IMAGE CREDITS